A 3-HOUR COPYWRITING PRACTICAL CLASS (BEGINNERS-ADVANCED)

BECOME A COPYWRITING EXPERT WITH THIS HANDBOOK

BY

ANTHONY A. BONAVENTURE

TABLE OF CONTENT

INTRODUCTION

I used to be a nobody, but copywriting skills changed my life. I used to be very broke back in the day. It's always very difficult for me to fend for myself because of the kind of jobs I did, which paid me a meager salary. Before, I could think of paying rent, sending a little money to my mom, and, of course, feeding (nobody is talking about wearing proper clothing). I would have spent my salary even before payday. So, it wasn't enough for me to live on. I was always calling relatives and friends for one help or the other. And at a point, they got tired of me. Some of my family and friends even started calling me names like "deadbeat," "a failure, "a parasite," and the list goes on.

That was when I decided not to continue my life in such a way. I was searching for something I could lay my hands on that would fetch me extra income. I wasn't even looking for something huge (because of the mindset that I had already developed, because of crushed confidence and lowered self-esteem); I just needed something extra to augment my salary. To cut a long story short, I stumbled into online business. It was a do-or-die for me. Either I hit my breakthrough via online business or I die trying, I said to myself. For two good years, I didn't make a dime; I was jumping from one online business to another, and that was my mistake. I was not focused. The hardest part was that my bills kept increasing, and I needed capital to buy courses and also pay my bills. While I was at it, I had to take a loan from my workplace to buy courses and set myself up. At the end of the month, I was only entitled to little or nothing. I was in serious depth, and I wasn't making any money. I was so depressed. I won't sleep all night because I will be doing research and I have to go to work the next morning. I considered taking my life at a certain point because things were very difficult. Life was like hell, and I felt like quitting. But the only thing that kept me moving despite all the odds was because of my mom. My mom kept on supporting me, she believed so much in me. It was at this moment that I stumbled on a course: "a copywriting course." I started the training and joined their students' online platform. It was on that platform, and I first read messages from others that they were making money. The more I read those messages, the more I became motivated, and I said to myself, if these people can make money through this skill, what is stopping me from doing the same? I was so determined and focused. I took my time in learning the ropes. Today, the rest is history. I have like three different online business brands. I still consult on contracts for many email marketing agencies around the world. And sometimes I take on a few copywriting freelance jobs if the price is right. My mom is now well taken care of. Housing is no longer an issue. I work from the convince of my home on my schedule. And I go on vacation whenever I feel like it. The list is endless. Glory be to God. It is from this comfort that I crafted this copywriting course for you. I have had great success stories with this skill for 25 years now. So, I decided to put this skill down in a book so that I could share my knowledge with newbies and professionals alike. As the saying goes, there's always room for improvement, so read and improve your skills, or read and learn a new skill.

With this practical book, you can go from a newbie to a professional in a matter of hours. Professionals can improve their skills in a matter of hours, too. The marketing departments of companies or firms can use it for training or retraining their marketing staff. Social media advertising managers can use it to improve their service, giving them a holistic view of a sales funnel. For those who want to work remotely from anywhere in the world, this is also your chance to turn the tables. And lots more. Getting this book is like procuring a gold mine, and like the gold mine, the potential is indeed limitless.

The above having been said; let's get on with the first item on the list, which is what copywriting is.

Note: The examples that will be used in this practical workbook are not live copies, as the products used are not real products. They're just samples or templates to help you comprehend better, and in writing live copy, more creativity should be employed, especially on the headline or subject lines.

Copywriting: What Is It?

Writing compelling marketing and promotional content that encourages readers to take action—like buying something, clicking on a link, donating to a cause, or scheduling a consultation—is known as copywriting.

Written advertisements that are published online or in print are also included in this content. Spoken content like scripts for TV shows or advertisements may also be included.

Since the language in these documents is referred to as "copy," that's where the term copywriting comes in.

Even though you may not know it, copywriting is used everywhere.

Indeed, a simple place to start is your email, where you may see many clear instances of copywriting. Copywriting may be seen in sales letters for different goods and services, fundraising letters from charity organizations, catalogs, and promotions for neighborhood eateries.

Examples of copywriting from four direct-mail package snippets

However, copywriting is much more than just writing for print.

You may find copywriting on most websites, free studies you download, and even the emails you get after registering for an account. Most internet content is written by copywriters.

Websites often display several calls to action

You see that some pages are written and structured in a manner that encourages you to behave in certain ways. Either "Read More," "Get Started," or "Follow Us" on social media is what is requested of you.

Every day, we see these straightforward online questions, which are all examples of compelling copywriting.

It's possible that what you hear is copywriting in action.

Spoken copywriting is used in TV ads, YouTube product evaluations, and even the brief "how-to" videos that demonstrate how to use a product.

This gives you a sense of the numerous ways that copywriting affects many aspects of our lives; we'll go into much more depth about the various forms of copywriting later.

NOTE: The term "copyright" should not be confused with copywriting. The unique legal right to sell or reproduce someone else's creative work, including music, literature, and artwork, is known as copyright. A copyright is meant to safeguard the original work and stop unauthorized use of it. Copyright is denoted by the © sign.

A Copywriter Is Who?

The professional writer in charge of crafting the language used in marketing and promotional materials is known as a copywriter.

You may have heard several misconceptions about authors, such as the notion that writing is innate and that it is not something that can be "learned."

Or maybe you've heard the opposite—that everyone can write and that it requires no special talent.

Both of these misconceptions when applied to copywriting; are false.

Copywriters are experts in their field who have studied and honed their trade. Although none of us are born with the ability to create flawless copy, almost everyone can pick up the talent with enough perseverance.

Copywriting has remained a somewhat restricted career that not many people enter, maybe because of the misconceptions about writers.

However, because skilled copywriters are in high demand, this benefits you as a copywriter.

Copywriters' high worth is also maintained by their exclusivity.

Warning: you don't need to have a long list of letters after your name to work as a highly compensated copywriter!

I assure you that you can quickly become operational with little expenditure.

Copywriters: Who Uses Them?

Writing copy is the foundation of almost all businesses.

Businesses wouldn't manage to reach out to new clients to broaden their markets or stay in touch with existing ones if they didn't have copywriters.

Websites, organizations that are nonprofit-based, service providers, and physical merchants all fall under this category.

Everybody uses and needs copywriters.

Use Apple Inc. as an example. You will see product descriptions if you go through their website.

Copywriters compose product descriptions, but you'll also note that there's always a link to a product video at the bottom of the page.

Who authored the video's script, you ask? Yes, you guessed correctly—a copywriter.

Apple uses copywriters extensively, as seen in the product videos, product descriptions, and other marketing materials.

Similar to Apple Inc., a large number of Fortune 500 corporations also employ copywriters. They have large marketing expenditures, and copywriters will get a share of those funds directly.

Nevertheless, if working for Fortune 500 firms isn't your thing, you're not required to.

Copywriters are also employed by a wide range of different businesses, large and small, including:

Investment companies and financial organizations

Pharmaceutical and medical supplies firms

producers of food

Non-governmental entities

Local service providers include hair salons and auto mechanics

Personal development, fitness, and other categories of coaches

Physicians, dentists, and other healthcare professionals

Self-help writers and presenters

manufacturers of dietary supplements and other supplementary medical goods

These are just a few examples of the kinds of companies that need your expertise as a professional copywriter.

There's a good chance that the copywriting sector has a position that perfectly matches your talents, regardless of your background or personal interests.

What distinguishes content writing from copywriting?

Some sites that you may read or hear may argue that content writing and copywriting are two separate things.

There is some validity to this, but we'll explain when this differentiation begins to fall apart.

Generally speaking, writing marketing and promotional content is referred to as copywriting. Contrarily, content writing is the process of creating editorial or informational pages for websites, including product pages, blog entries, and article pages.

Each term's definition is accurately stated here.

However, other definitions contend that content writing is not copywriting because it is only informational and does not include persuasion.

Almost every webpage will have a call to action or some sort of persuasiveness to it.

This is especially noticeable on a product page if the bottom has a prominent **"Buy Now!"** button.

Even an article page, however, employs subliminal calls to action, typically in the form of recommendations for other pages on the website or connections to other resources.

Every one of these has a persuasive aspect.

Therefore, it is incorrect to say that copywriting and content writing are different.

Content writing, in my opinion, is just another kind of copywriting.

In addition, content writing, like any effective copywriting, seeks to captivate readers and compel them to act, even if that action is as simple as remaining on a website to view further pages.

Is The Copywriting Industry Growing?

To put it succinctly, sure. For many years, copywriting has been researched and acknowledged as a crucial component of marketing.

However, copywriting has a far longer history. Vendors on the streets of ancient Rome undoubtedly had to utilize persuasion while negotiating with possible clients.

Furthermore, when did Van Camp's Boston Baked Pork and Beans advertisement debut?

Van Camp's Ham and Beans was advertised in 1897. It would be easy to presume that the advertisement debuted in the 1980s or even the 1970s. In fact, the Ladies' Home Journal published it for the first time in 1897.

I intend to convey the idea that copywriting is a very old profession that is here to stay.

Reaching out to new clients and clearly communicating what they can provide has always been a requirement for businesses.

In the era of digital information, this is even more crucial. People nowadays are exposed to an increasing number of conflicting messages from various media.

All businesses need to differentiate themselves from the competition, which is why a lot of them spend a lot of money on marketing and copywriting.

The data below demonstrates how copywriting is a crucial component of the majority of contemporary organizations, both online and in print:

Currently, 56% of US businesses employ traditional direct-mail packages, which are delivered to customers' homes.

In the upcoming year, 81% of these businesses want to continue using direct mail or perhaps expand upon it.

Online content marketing is used by 90% of all firms in the digital sphere.

Businesses are actively engaging in content marketing in 70% of cases, and 53% anticipate increasing their content marketing budget in 2024 compared to 2023.

The creation of their internet content is outsourced by over 67% of organizations. Stated differently, they use outside copywriters.

According to a recent survey by Robert Half International, the need for competent copywriters is growing as more businesses need to provide engaging material for print and web-based campaigns. Copywriters will be among the new hires, according to 60% of advertising and marketing professionals.

For copywriters and those of us fortunate enough to work in the field, the future appears bright.

Let's now quickly contrast this with other industries. The U.S. Bureau of Labor Statistics reports that 190 of the 808 jobs it tracks are expected to fall in the ensuing eight years.

This implies that around 25%, or one-quarter, of all professions in the United States will see employment losses! Professionals from many backgrounds, including auto mechanics, CEOs, electronics engineers, pharmacists, and farm workers, are included in this.

By 2032, there will likely be 17,900 fewer jobs in even a field like computer programming, where the minimum requirement for entry is a bachelor's degree. This represents a 7% reduction in employment.

Businesses require copywriting, a highly sought-after skill, to thrive. Because of this, copywriting is a lucrative and virtually endlessly productive sector that is expanding.

You will always be in demand and able to take advantage of the high income and stability that come with being a copywriter as long as you put in the work to study the trade. Having stated that, let's get started.

Module 1:

Reasons Why People Buy

In this module, you learn that people would rather spend money on their wants rather than on their needs. Stated below are the reasons why people buy:

1. To make money

2. To save money

3. To save time

4. To avoid effort

5. To achieve better health

6. To feel happy and confident

7. To gain praise and feel popular or smart

8. To avoid physical or mental pain

9. To feel loved

Your service must be able to meet one or more of the above. The more it meets the customers' wants, the easier it becomes to convince people to buy your product/service.

"WHO" IS YOUR COPY ABOUT?

Since your customers only care about how you can help them, you should do the following:

·   Convince them that you know their problem.

·   Tell them that you feel and know their pains.

·   Tell them that you have the solution.

·   It is only when they are convinced that you know their problems, pains, and struggles then they will listen to you.

·   When they are listening to you; remember that they still have doubts (this is because other service providers tell them the same things you are telling them now)

·   It is now that you bring in your testimonials to prove your authenticity.

·   Then the evidence of what your services can do will be your selling points.

NOTE: Please whatever you do avoid using the word "I" and make your whole copy about "you" that is your customers. Therefore, your copy should be about your customers and not yourself.

Module 2:

What You Need to Write a Great Copy

The below are the eleven information you need to write a sales copy successfully. Whether you are writing your sales copy or writing for a client.

1.   Name of the product/service

2.   The benefits of the product/service

3.   Features and/or components of the product or service

4.   What makes you stand out

5.   What pains does your product or service remove

6.   Research data to back your claims

7.   Social proof or proof of authority.

8.   Frequently asked questions.

9.   Testimonials And Case Studies.

10. Bonuses.

11. Who Are Your Target Audience?

More Details On The Above:

1.   Name Of The Product/Service.

You must know the name of the product or service you're selling.

2.   The Benefit Of The Product/Service.

People are going to buy your products and services because of how it is going to benefit them. So, the stronger the benefits the better your copy will sell. Therefore, find a way of aligning the benefits of your product or service to the core wants of people.

3.   Features And/Or Components Of The Product Or Service.

For each feature you mention, you should know how it benefits your customers or how it connects to the customers' wants.

4.   What Makes You Stand Out?

Should be; something that you offer that other similar service providers don't offer. Don't use words like "Best product ever or best quality" since everybody claims to be the best. Instead say the exact thing that makes your products or services unique maybe something like; a faster delivery time or something of that sort etc. And always remember to connect it to the wants of your customers.

5.	What Pains Does Your Product Or Service Remove?

Clearly point out the pains your customers are going through as a result of not using your services. State the client's situation, struggles, and pain. This is because being able to state their problems means you understand what their problems are. Then pitch your product or service after that. This also implies that you can help them solve their issues.

6.	Research Data To Back Up Your Claims.

Make sure you research on the internet to find proven facts to back up your claims. It will make your claims believable.

7.	Social Proof Or Proof Of Authority.

The following are what you can use as social proof or proof of authority:

- Have you had practical success with your services,

·   Have you been featured in any magazine, news, blog, or the like,

·   Do you have certifications relevant to your industry

·   Has an authority in your field ever mentioned you?

8.   Frequently Asked Questions.

Here you will think about all the objections your clients may have about your products or services. You can Google the FAQ of your already established competitors and tweak it to suit your product or service. But after that remember to ask for customers' feedback and testimonials when you start making sales.

9.   Testimonials And Case Studies.

The more testimonials you have the better your copy will convert and sell. And if by any means you don't have testimonials, give out your product or service for free or at low cost for people to use in exchange for testimonials.

10. Bonuses.

Include bonuses or free gifts that are related to your product or service and it should be valuable of course, to your customers.

11. Who Are Your Target Audience?

Make sure you find out who your target audience is including their:

- Age range

- Pain points

- Their mentality

- Then who finances the purchase (is it them or someone else, this is based on the product and the age range you're selling to).

Module 3:

Copywriting Formulas That Work

If you Google copywriting formulas, you will see a lot of them. But for the sake of this work, we will be using these formulas. This is because they are the traditional copywriting formulas. They are the foundation upon which other formulas came, and they are:

1.   Before-After-Bridge

2.   Attention Interest Desire Action (AIDA)

3.   Problem Agitate Solution (PAS)

4.   Bridge-After-Bridge

Let's look at the above in details and also give practical examples.

1. Before-After-Bridge

Talk about the current situation of your audience, then talk about where they desire to be, and then end it with how they will get that desire.

Example:

Is this you?

You know that being active on social media is going to help your brand

You've learned that you should be posting every day to keep your audience glued to your brand

But you're confused about what to write daily to get the best engagements

You make some posts, but the engagement is poor

Now, what if you could sit back and concentrate on your business while we take the pain of coming up with super-engaging content for your audience…

…content that will have your followers engaging, and taking up your offers crazily?

Isn't this what you want?

If you answered YES, then click here, and let's discuss how we can help you achieve that.

2.   AIDA (Attention Interest, Desire Action)

This formula gets the attention of the targeted audience, piques their interest then shows them their desire and tells them to take action.

Example:

Over a million people out there are hoping to do business with you

Yes, millions of people within your target audience are on Facebook and Instagram, and they are ready to hear from you, and even buy what you have to sell

All you have to do is create great content that will resonate with them, and they will literally flip their wallet and pay you

Would you want such content?

3.   PAS (Problem Agitate Solution)

Here hit their pain points, exacerbate the problem, and then provide them with your solution.

Example:

Writing your own marketing sales copy is difficult

You'd open your computer and spend hours on the computer staring at a blank screen and confused about where to start

Hours pass to says, and you end with a copy you think is good enough

You spend time and money driving traffic to the copy, hoping to get sales

But nothing happens

Only a few persons click your ads, and none of them buys

You get frustrated and you decide to hire a copywriter to redo the entire copy for you

But he's charging you a thousand dollars for just one copy

And you actually don't have that much cash to spare

You get frustrated, and you start contemplating to quit

Stop! Don't do it!

There's an easier, better, and cost-effective way to have all your sales copy written for you in minutes…

…copy that can bring you loads of clicks and massive sales

You will achieve this without hiring a copywriter or spending days starring on a blank computer screen

CopyDyno is going to handle all this for you in minutes

<u>To see how it works Click on the video below</u>

4.   Bridge-After-Bridge

Talk about what your audience desires, talk about others who are enjoying that desire, and then how to get that desire.

Example:

Just imagine this for a second

You just created a solid product and you're eager to have people buy it, because you know it'll help them

So, you set up a Facebook campaign for it and fire it up

And in 24 hours, your inbox is filled with countless orders…far more than you can handle

Your bank account is reverberating with credit alert notifications, and you're happy

Wait!!!

This looks like a fantasy...too good to be true, right?

But it's actually possible when you do things the right way

In fact, the scenario I painted above is exactly what one of our clients Mauris from Texas is experiencing

He has more clients than he can handle right now

And that was possible for him because he went about the campaign and promotion the right way

What's the right way? You'd be asking

The right way is to work with experts to identify your ideal customers

And then targeting them through Facebook ads, with powerful copy written to turn strangers into paying customers

That's how Mauris did it, and if you follow the same process, you'll get the same results

Want the same experience as Marius?

<u>Then book a free call with us now and let's help you create a winning campaign that can</u>

<u>**bring you more customers than you can handle**</u>

Or

Want us to help you get more customers than you can handle this month?

Then, be like Marius who just closed his cart because he couldn't handle the many orders we're sending him

<u>**Book a free call with us today, to see how it works.**</u>

Note: The above examples are not live copies as the products used are not real products. They're just samples or temples to help you comprehend better.

Module 4:

How To Write An Attention-Grabbing Ad

What's an ad? An ad is a message that has been paid for to be publicized, and it's intended to convince people to take action.

The sole objective of an ad is to sell a click.

WHAT MAKES A GOOD AD?

- A good headline

· It must be congruent with your landing page

· Should stop people on their tracks

· Must have a value proposition that is worth a click

· You must have a clear yet simple call to action

HOW TO WRITE A GREAT AD

1. Headline

2. Body

3. Closing

HEADLINES

We're going to be looking at different ways of writing headlines in an ad.

Using Questions:

1.   Searching for an effective weight-loss formula?

2.   Looking to lose weight this summer?

3.   Want to crush that body fat in just a few days with these 3 amazing techniques?

Using numbers:

1.   5 ways to lose weight… Even with 6 kids

2.   7 weight loss strategies that work in 2024

3.   3 workout plans that burn 10 lbs in 5 days

4.   3 diets that Are Slowly Killing You

5.   3 miracle weight loss techniques for 2024

6.   48 hours of skin transformation

Inspire Curiosity:

1.   I lost 22 lbs on a keto diet. The recipes I used will surprise you

2.   5 shocking ways to lose weight revealed No. 3 will shock you

3.	Is a low-fat diet dangerous? Find out if you're putting your health on the line.

4.	3 diets that Are Slowly Killing You

5.	The opposite sex thinks you have STDs because of these.

6.	...3 days Skin transformation: this product will surprise you

Benefits:

1.	The ultimate guide to losing weight and becoming healthier

2.	Lose 7 lbs in 7 days, get your dream body, and regain your confidence

Testimonial:

1.	"I lost 13 lbs in a week with these strategies"—John Cliff

2.	"These fat-burning formulas flat out work" Sandra May

Social Proof:

1.   How to burn fat and get the ripped body of Dwayne Johnson

2.   How to lose weight like Adele

3.   How Rick Ross burnt down his body fats in 90 days

Interweaving headline formulas:

1.   7 ways to lose weight and become healthier, like Adele

2.   3 amazing muscle-gain techniques Jordan Davis used in Creed

This is the use of numbers, benefits, and social proof.

BODY OF YOUR AD COPY.

State what your ad is promoting and how it can help improve lives (keep it short and simple).

Examples:

Sample. 1.

We've compiled the most effective weight-loss techniques into a short guide.

With this guide, you'll be able to:

Lose up to 14 lbs every week

Look younger and feel great

Stop starving and avoiding the delicious food you love the most

Get the sexy, lean body of Dwayne Johnson

Achieve a complete health transformation

It contains only 25 pages, so you can easily read and understand it.

Eg.2. (AIDA Attention Interest Desire Action)

There are hundreds of celebrities who lost weight using this rare but amazing technique

All you have to do is download this weight loss guide and start losing that excess fat.

Or

The FDA and Intertek in 2015 certified that this product doesn't just clear dark/dead skin, and rashes… but is also 100% safe

All you have to do to get that clear clean skin you deserve is to get your hands on this amazing product

Eg.3. (Bridge–After–Bridge)

Want to lose 60 lbs in 30 days?

Then be like Paulin who just lost 60 lbs in 30 days, despite her busy schedule, with our 3 miracle techniques.

Or

3 days of shocking skin transformation therapy

Just imagine having your skin toned like that of your favorite celebrities

Janice one of our clients got her skin glowing in just 3 days despite how bad her skin was

Eg.4. (PAS Problem Agitate Solution)

We have compiled 9 harmful diets that contain bad fat and are slowly killing you.

Numbers 3, 6, and 9 are the worst of them all.

Or

The rashes, dark spots, and dead skin have your skin looking bad already.

The worst is that the opposite sex thinks that you're covered in STDs because of them

Eg.5. (Before-After-Bridge)

Having difficulty losing excess and stubborn body fat?

I'm sure you want to look amazingly hot with the perfect body of a model.

What if I told you that you can get your desired body in a matter of days with these amazing 3 techniques?

Or

Watching your skin darken and lose its smoothness?

I'm sure it's a very bad experience for you

And I'm also sure that you want to gain that fair, smooth, and silky skin of a model...right?

What if I told you that you are one click away from getting your desired skin tone in just 48 hours

THE CALL TO ACTION

Stated below are the different variations of Call to Action:

Adding numbers:

It may be discount-based or the number of things you are given out.

1.   Order today and get a 75% discount

2.   Click here to get my top 7 keto recipes!

Adding Adjectives:

It provokes emotions because they describe the quality/quantity of your product or services.

1.   Order now and we'll ship your beautiful dress to you

2.   Click here to get this gorgeous wig today!

Make a Promise:

1.   Click Here to lose 10 lbs in 1 week

2.   Start losing weight now

Using Fear of Missing Out:

Creating Artificial Scarcity

1.   Sales end tomorrow, Get yours Now!

2.   Today only: Get 50% off

3.   Order today and get a 50% discount

Simple call-to-action:

1.   By just clicking on this link now

Interweaving the call to action:

1.   Click here to gain an amazing skin transformation in a matter of days with a whopping 75% discount.

2.   Click here to get that amazing skin transformation you desire in 3 days quarantined: with a whopping 75% discount.

You can fuse the above Headlines, Bodies, and Call-to-action and you will get a complete ad copy.

Note: The above examples are not live copies as the products used are not real products. They're just samples or temples to help you comprehend better.

Module 5:

Writing A Landing Page Copy

What Is A Landing Page:

A landing page is the first page your ideal customers land on when they click on your advert.

It's the second step in a sales funnel. It may be a sales page, a product description page, an about us page, an opt-in page, or any other page on a website or wherever your customers land. Furthermore, if you link the advert to your About Us page, sales page, or any other page, that page automatically becomes your landing page.

Here is something weird, the traditional thing is to link your advert to your lead capture page: which is a page where people will have to key in their phone number or their email to get something (a freebie, lead magnet, etc.) from you. This means the function of a landing page is to help the customers fill in their information to get a gift (lead magnet) from you.

Lead magnet: is what people get for free in exchange for their contact information. It could be a free PDF report, video tutorial, audio, an app, a newsletter, or even a case study. This must be of high value, easy to use, must be related to what you're selling or advertising, and must solve a specific problem that your customers are having.

TIPS ON CREATING A LANDING PAGE COPY

· It should not be lengthy and it should be straight to the point

- It must not try to sell

- Should have 5 elements

- Headline

- Bullet point

- Video

- Social proof

- Big call to action.

THE HEADLINE: the headline of a landing page spells out the value you're going to give away for free. (And it's the most important part of the landing page) and just like a sales letter, the headline section must consist of 3 parts:

- The Eyebrow (the eyebrow

- The main headline

- The sub-headline.

Examples:

Eyebrow:

1. Attention: all overweight people who have given up on their weight loss journey.

2. If you're tired of trying every weight loss product that ends up not working, read this

3 Ways To Write A Powerful Headline For Your Landing Page

1.   The "How To X Without Y" Formula (How To Lose 30 Lbs Without Starving Yourself)

2.   The "X Ways To Y in Z" Formula (3 Ways To Lose 10 Lbs In 30 Days)

3.   The "Who Else Wants To" Formula (Who Else Wants To Lose 10 Lbs Without Dieting)

Main Headline:

Example:

1.   This Brand New Guide Reveals 5 Simple Exercises That Have Helped Me And Thousands Of Other People To Burn Down 60 Lbs in 30 Days.

Sub-headline: it backs up the claim you made in the main headline. It can also boost clarity or boost the benefits of your freebie or talk about what makes the freebie unique.

Example:

1.   These exercises have been proven to give shocking results without having to step into the gym, even if you have a very busy schedule.

IF WE JOIN THEM TOGETHER YOU WILL GET SOMETHING LIKE THIS:

Attention: All Overweight People Who Have Given Up On Their Weight Loss Journey

This Brand New Guide Reveals 5 Simple Exercises That Have Helped Me And Thousands Of Other People To Burn Down 60 Lbs in 30 Days.

These Exercises Have Been Proven To Give Shocking Results Without Having To Step

**Into The Gym, Even If You've Very Busy
Schedules.**

The above is a complete sample of a landing
page headline.

Bullet points:

In this section, you're going to list the features
and benefits of your lead magnet. Here you have
to look into the results your readers really want
that your lead magnet can help them to achieve
then you magnify the value to sound so
irresistible that anyone who lands on the page
will get the lead magnet. Furthermore, don't just
list the features of your lead magnet intertwine
with its benefits too.

Examples:

Inside this guide, you'll discover:

·   How to burn fat, slim down, and get sexy
without interrupting your already busy days

·   The exact strategies you must be using if you
want to get into shape fast

·   One simple technique that can flush 2 lbs of
fat out of your body every day

·   How to make exercising so much fun that you'll want to do it every minute of the day

·   One small little item you must have if you don't want to spend an hour a day at the gym

And so much more

NOTE: (Always remember to keep your landing page short. This means that you should limit your bullet points to 4 or 5 no matter how many they are and remember to choose the best of the best 4 or 5 benefits and features for your bullet points).

Another Element of a landing page (THE VIDEO)

Remember that this element is optional, so if you don't have it, your landing page will still work. If you don't have a video use a fitting image for it. However, adding a video to your landing page will boost engagement and increase the conversion rate of the page. So what type of video should have on your landing page?

3 Types Of Videos You Can Use On Your Landing Page

1.   Explainer video

2.   Product demonstration video

3.   Testimonial video

We are not going to learn how to write a video script here, because there is a full module below that talks about video scripts.

Have These In Mind When Creating Your Landing Page Videos

·   Keep the video short

·   Place the video above the fold

·   At the end of the video, a call to action should be included.

The Last Element of Your Landing Page Copy.

The Call-To-Action: This is the exact instruction you give to your readers to follow for them to get your lead magnet. Remember that the best call-to-actions are commands; here you have to sound authoritative when telling your readers what to do. Your call-to-action must also be crystal clear, it must make a single specific request and it must let your readers know exactly what to do to get the lead magnet.

Example:

Best of all, I'm giving away the entire guide 100% free.

<u>**Enter your best email below to receive the eBook link.**</u>

The Full sample of a landing page copy:

Attention: All Overweight People Who Have Given Up On Their Weight Loss Journey

This Brand-New Guide Reveals 5 Simple Exercises That Have Helped Me And Thousands Of Other People To Burn Down 60 Lbs in 30 Days.

These Exercises Have Been Proven To Give Shocking Results Without Having To Step Into The Gym, Even If You've Very Busy Schedules.

Inside this guide, you'll discover:

· How to burn fat, slim down, and get sexy without interrupting your already busy days

· The exact strategies you must be using if you want to get into shape fast

· One simple technique that can flush 2 lbs of fat out of your body every day

· How to make exercising so much fun that you'll want to do it every minute of the day

· One small little item you must have if you don't want to spend an hour a day at the gym

And so much more.

Best of all, I'm giving away the entire guide 100% free.

<u>Enter your best email below to receive the eBook link.</u>

Note: The above examples are not live copies as the products used are not real products. They're just samples or temples to help you comprehend better.

Module 6:

Writing Sales Copy That Converts

Elements Of A High-Converting Sales Page

The headline: This is the most important part of this copy. This is because, the tone and mood set by the headline, will likely determine if the visitor will go ahead and read the rest of your page or just exit from that point.

How To Write A Good Headline

- Eyebrow

- Headline

- Sub-headline

The eyebrow: This is not compulsory but very important because it gets the attention of your audience and gets them to read the main headline; this part calls out the particular audience your sales copy is made for.

Example:

1.   For Everyone Who's Been Unsuccessful in Trying To Lose Weight

2.   Attention: All Overweight People Who Have Given Up On Their Weight Loss Journey

3.   If You Are On The Verge Of Giving Up On Your Weight Loss Quest, This Is For You

Headline: The best way to write a great headline is to make a bold claim of what your product or service will do for your audience. You can do this by stating their most burning problem and providing them with its solution and of course, this can be done with just one sentence.

HOW TO MAKE YOUR HEADLINES MORE POWERFUL

· Using Numbers In Headlines

· Story Telling Technique

· Using Warnings

· Words That Trigger Curiosity in Headlines like:

> "Shocking", " Must", "Revealed", "Exposed", " Secret", "Confession", " Won't Tell", "Horror", " Alarming", etc.

Example:

1. How To Shed 60 Lbs In 30 Days Without Fasting Or Visiting The Gym

2.	Even If Every Other Method Has Failed You, This Weird Technique Will Help You Shed 60 Lbs In 30 Days– Guaranteed!

3.	Finally Revealed: The Weird Technique That Burns Down 60 Lbs in 30 Days – No Fasting, Or Hitting The Gym

4.	Exposed! 5 Weird Methods To Lose Weight Without Fasting Or Hitting The Gym – No 3 Will Shock You!

5.	A Previously Obese Truck Driver Shares How He Lost 60 Lbs in 30 Days

6.	How A Truck Driver Went From 270 Lbs To 190 Lbs In 30 Days Without Exercising Or Going On Diet

7.	WARNING: These Popular Fruits Could Be Making You Add 10 Lbs Everyday

The Sub-headline:

The sub-headline backs up the claim you made on the headline or just makes them relax to listen further by dropping some social proof or by reemphasizing how effective and easy it is to make use of your product/service.

Example:

(Let's pick an eyebrow, headline, and back it up with a sub-headline)

Attention: All Overweight People Who Have Given Up On Their Weight Loss Journey

Finally Revealed: The Weird Technique That Burns Down 60 Lbs in 30 Days – No Fasting, Or Hitting The Gym

…Even A Busy Truck Driver That's Always On The Road, Used It To Go From 280 Lbs To 170 Lbs In 40 Days

(Put a Call-to-action immediately after the Headline.)

Example:

<u>Gain Access To Secret Technique Now</u>

Bullet points: are meant to cause even more intrigue for the reader, and highlight your benefits as well. It should inspire curiosity and the WOW factor in your copy.

Examples:

(Make sure to infuse the reasons why people buy see module 1)

· Get that perfect shape that gets the opposite sex drooling

· Works fast, with no side effect

· Used by busy persons with no time for the gym

· Approved by FDA

· Tons of testimonials from buyers

(Put a call to action immediately after the bullet points)

Example:

<u>Lose Weight With This Technique Now</u>

[Drop 3 - 4 Testimonials Here]

(Put a call to action immediately after the testimonials.)

Example:

<u>Get Your Access To This Secret Technique And Start Losing Weight Now</u>

Here Use The PAS Formula (see module 3)

Example:

(These are single questions)

Do you want to lose weight?

Have you been struggling to shed off excess fat, but nothing is working?

Are you ready to burn fat so you can get that sexy lean body you desire?

OR

(Multiple questions: try and make your copy conversational)

Dear Friend,

Let me ask a few questions:

Are you tired of being overweight no matter what you try?

Fed up with counting calories, taking dangerous weight loss pills, endless starvation, sweating in the gym, and avoiding the food you love, in the name of dieting?

Have you often envied slim people and the way they seem to easily get everybody's attention, have loads of fun in what they do, and attract the opposite sex like crazy?

Here; exacerbate the problem with a short story (note: don't over-exacerbate the problem since it can cause the reader to exit your sales page. Be mild)

Well, you're not alone

Over 70% of US adults are struggling with excess fat

And just like you, millions more all over the world are struggling to lose weight

And the number keeps increasing every day

But that doesn't mean that you have to keep putting up with this problem

Because being overweight can make your life increasingly difficult

I'm sure that it's preventing you from wearing the clothes you fancy just because they won't fit

It has stopped you from feeling comfortable, attractive, and confident

And you now look ugly, unfit, and unhealthy

Right?

I'm also sure that you're always tired and don't have energy to do the things you feel like doing

Not to mention the fact that people may be laughing at you. They may even call you "Biggy" or some other funny names

You may start to avoid social situations so you don't get mocked

And you may even be at risk of developing life-threatening health issues like diabetes, cholesterol, and other metabolic diseases.

Here back it up with proofs

Worse still, excess body fat can take your life

I'm not saying this to frighten you, I'm saying it because it's the true

Being overweight is linked to heart disease and early death in people, both with or without a history of cardiovascular disease

This finding came from a new study conducted by researchers from one of the top universities in America

Over 65,000 subjects without known heart diseases at the start of the study, were involved in the investigation

During a follow-up that ended in June 2017, 7,885 of them were admitted to the hospital for heart diseases

And during a second follow-up that ended in December 2017, 2,304 subjects died

Results showed that the people with excess body fat and without known cardio diseases had a relative 35% greater risk of heart diseases and a relatively 93% elevated chance of early death, compared to those without excess body fat

The reason for this is simple:

Being overweight can lead to fatty materials building up in your arteries that carry blood to your heart. And that can damage and clog the artery, leading to heart attack

What does that mean to you?

It means that if you are overweight now, you're at risk of serious heart disease and even early death

Here You Introduce your solution

Fortunately, there's something you can do to lose weight, get your dream body prevent all the problems listed above

So, panic no more!

What exactly is it? You may ask

Well, I'm a weight loss expert who has helped thousands of men and women to achieve their weight loss goals.

For the first time, I have decided to create a one-of-a-kind blueprint for people who want to lose fat, keep it off, and build their confidence.

Now, the good thing about this blueprint is that you don't have to go to the gym and no equipment is needed. The workout it contains can be done at home using only your body weight. So, no equipment is needed.

Another thing that sets the blueprint apart from other similar products is that it is designed specifically for people like you

I'm talking about adults who don't like dieting

Plus, those who are busy and have very little time to engage in traditional workout routines

That's the major reason a busy truck driver who's always on the road, used it to lose 72 lbs in 40 days

Most importantly, you won't have to wait for months to lose weight with the exercises, workout, and meal plans in this blueprint.

You can start seeing results as soon as 48 hours from the day you started.

With that said, let me tell you more about my weight loss blueprint and how you can take advantage of it

Introducing…

My ADULT FAT SHRINKER weight loss guide

· **"ADULT FAT SHRINKER"** is a step-by-step blueprint that shows you exactly how to get real results within a short time by using my unique and revolutionary ways to lose weight

· This blueprint is packed with the most effective workout routines you can do at home with your body weight.

· You'll not just read about the workout. Instead, you'll watch me do them (I'll include videos).

·   The blueprint will also show you insider tips and techniques that will help you burn fat easily and without starving yourself or engaging in the strenuous exercises you hate.

·   You'll discover the 3 major lies that food manufacturing companies, weight loss MLM, and many so-called certified gym trainers tell you about belly weight loss. Lies that are designed to keep you overweight so you will continue to buy their products.

·   You'll understand the reason you haven't lost weight even though you've been exercising and dieting.

·   Every other thing you need to achieve your weight loss goals is included. This means that you'll also get meal plans that include a full grocery list and recipes (vegetarian or regular options)

·   You'll also get daily coaching on other aspects (outside nutrition and workouts) that may hinder your fat-loss goals

·   Plus you'll get access to my private Facebook group where I'll answer any questions you may have. You'll also meet like-minded women and men who motivate and cheer you to success.

· There's no need to go to the gym; no equipment is needed and no guesswork on what exercises to do and how many reps or sets.

· You'll be able to lose up to 2 lbs per day with the secret system exposed inside this blueprint. Best of all, it doesn't involve unhealthy drugs or pills that make you put on fat instead of losing it (trust me, this happens quite often).

· You'll finally become proud of your body so you can exhibit it with total confidence whether you're in the gym, at the beach, or just about any place

· And it will supercharge your body and your stamina, so you will never feel lazy or low on energy!

· Finally, the result you'll get will make people of the opposite sex drool over you and beg for your attention (who doesn't want that?)

The bottom line is:

This blueprint has helped thousands of people like you to get real results, and I'm sure that it will help you too

Skeptical?

Don't just take my word for it

Here's what others are saying about this awesome blueprint

[Insert 3-4 testimonials here]

Here you make your offer (try and make it as irresistible as possible and again don't fake things that you know your product doesn't do. Note that the $ figures below are imaginary and only for this course. So, research and make sure you add real figures)

Would you like to achieve same or even better results?

The **"ADULT FAT SHRINKER"** is for you if your answer is yes.

But before I show you how to get access to the blueprint, let me quickly list everything that comes with it

They include:

·   A 12-hour video course packed with the most effective workout routines you can do at home to lose 2 pounds a day ($50)

·   Transcript of the course ($20)

·   Free access to all future updates to the information ($200)

·   Meal plans (and full grocery list and recipes) that show you exactly what to eat and what to avoid if you want to lose weight fast ($10)

·   Daily coaching on other aspects (outside of nutrition and workouts) that may hinder your fat loss goals ($100)

·   Access to my private Facebook group, where you'll meet with like-minded people who will motivate and cheer you to success

·   Lifetime access to ask me any question whenever you're stuck ($500)

Total ($880) in value.

But that's not all though…

Because I'm serious about helping you to lose weight and get your dream body fast, I'm making available these 3 powerful bonuses that will help you accelerate your results

- · Bonus 1: Describe, ($ value)

- · Bonus 2: Describe, ($ value)

- · Bonus 3: Describe, ($ value)

As you can see, the collective value of these bonuses is $XXX

But I'm going to give it to you for 100% free

However, you can only get them if you order **"ADULT FAT SHRINKER"** within the next 24 hours!

Here: reveal your price (try to introduce FOMO fear of missing out in your pricing, by adding a limited time frame to force them to take action).

These bonuses are just to reward people who take fast action - and so they will be removed by this time tomorrow

Now, you're probably wondering how much this guide is going to cost you, right?

Well, I could easily charge $500 for this powerful blueprint and sleep very well at night, because it's worth several times that. Heck, so many people sell courses that are not even as good as mine for double that price.

But I'm not going to charge you that much, and for a very good reason.

I care so much about your health. And I don't want money to be the reason you'll miss out on this blueprint.

So how much? Believe it or not…

I'm going to allow you to register at a discounted price of $49

However, I have limited the number of people I'll allow to get this course at this price.

And right now, I'm already getting to the limit, so this price won't stay for long. Once I reach that limit, I will increase the price to at least double what it is now.

So, make sure you get on board before the price increases.

Here: make your offer more irresistible by giving them a guarantee (by doing this you remove every risk from your reader; this is because people are always skeptical and don't want to lose money. Show them they're not going to lose any money).

(Put a call to action immediately after this section.)

Example:

<u>(Get Your Access Right Now)</u>

I am even going to make this crazy deal more complete by adding a 100% love-it-or-get-your-money-back guarantee!

With this guarantee, you're only gonna pay if you like my **"ADULT FAT SHRINKER"** weight loss guide.

What this means is that you can get this guide today, use it to lose weight, and get the attractive body you desire

If you like it, great. You exchanged a small amount of money for a large amount of value. Awesome!

If on the other hand, you think that this weight loss blueprint isn't worth your money…

…or if you don't like the level of results you get, just ask for a refund within 60 days and you'll get your money back

You will agree with me that this sounds more than fair, right?

Here: restate your offer as a reminder of what your offer is, its value, and what they will pay to get it.

To recap, here's a list of what you'll get when you order my "ADULT FAT SHRINKER" weight loss guide today:

·   A 12-hour video course packed with the most effective workout routines you can do at home to lose 2 pounds a day ($50)

·   Transcript of the course ($20)

·   Free access to all future updates to the information ($200)

·   Meal plans (and full grocery list and recipes) that show you exactly what to eat and what to avoid if you want to lose weight fast ($10)

·   Daily coaching on other aspects (outside of nutrition and workouts) that may hinder your fat loss goals ($100)

·   Access to my private Facebook group where you'll meet with like-minded people who will motivate and cheer you to success

·   Lifetime access to ask me any question whenever you're stuck ($500)

·   Bonus 1: Describe, ($ value)

·   Bonus 2: Describe, ($ value)

·   Bonus 3: Describe, ($ value)

TOTAL PRICE TODAY = ($1880)

WHAT YOU PAY TODAY = ($49)

Here, place a call to action immediately after restating your offer

Example:

GET YOUR ACCESS TODAY TO QUALIFY FOR ALL THE BONUSES

Here try to introduce the fear factor in the form of a warning.

Now you have two options:

Option A: You can get this blueprint today and begin to lose weight

Who knows…you could burn up to 60 lbs of excess body fat in 30 days like the guy who sent me his testimonial yesterday.

You'll unveil your sexy lean body.

You'll boost your immune system, reduce your risk of sickness, and combat tiredness and fatigue

You'll achieve optimum mental & physical performance

You'll skyrocket your energy level, your focus, productivity, and your confidence.

And you'll begin to feel attractive again

Option B: You can close this page now and go watch Netflix.

But if you do that, you will be stuck with that stubborn excess fat that has made your life miserable.

You'll be at risk of developing diabetes and heart disease.

People will continue to make fun of you and call you names whenever you go out.

You'll never wear the clothes and shoes you fancy because they won't fit.

You'll be at risk of losing your partner because nobody loves being with a fat person.

And you'll continue to waste your hard-earned money on weight loss products that don't work.

So which option are you going to take?

If you're ready to take action, choose option A…

Then click here to get instant access to my "ADULT FAT SHRINKER" weight loss guide today.

Regards

[Your Name And Credentials]

Here: add a postscript. (This should be a summary of the whole sales letter, stating your reader's problem, the solution, the offer, and the guarantee. If you used a scarcity in your sales letter remind your readers of the limited-time offer or quantity and then end it with a call-to-action)

Example:

PS: in case you had no time to read this letter word-by-word, here's a brief recap:

1.   I realized that so many people like you are struggling to lose weight. So, I put all my weight loss knowledge, tutorials, and video training into one comprehensive blueprint so that you can get all the information you need to know to achieve your weight loss goals.

As soon as you say 'yes' to this course, you will get instant access to the following:

2.   A 12-hour video course packed with the most effective workout routines you can do at home to lose 2 pounds a day ($50)

3.   Transcript of the course ($20)

4.   Free access to all future updates to the information ($200)

5.   Meal plans (and full grocery list and recipes) that show you exactly what to eat and what to avoid if you want to lose weight fast ($10)

6.   Daily coaching on other aspects (outside of nutrition and workouts) that may hinder your fat loss goals ($100)

7.   Access to my private Facebook group where you'll meet with like-minded people who will motivate and cheer you to success

8.   Lifetime access to ask me any question whenever you're stuck ($500)

9.   Bonus 1: Describe, ($ value)

10. Bonus 2: Describe, ($ value)

11. Bonus 3: Describe, ($ value)

And so much more.

12. These training and bonuses have helped and are still helping a lot of people like you to lose

up to 61 lbs in 30 days. That's why I'm 100%
sure that they will work for you too.

13. Normally, I charge a little over $XX for this
comprehensive blueprint. However, all you'll
pay to get it today is a measly $XX.

And there is no catch to this offer. There's No
hidden fee to pay and no compulsory upsell to
purchase.

Best of all, you are fully covered with my 100%
money-back guarantee. If you're not happy with
the blueprint for any reason, simply get back to
me and I'll be happy to refund every penny you
paid ASAP.

14. Finally, I just know you're going to love this
blueprint. Yet, because the discount I'm offering
yours is time-limited, I'm afraid if you don't act
right now, you may miss out.

15. To be precise, I'm running this promo as a
one-week marketing test. And the test period is
already coming to an end after this test, I may
pull his offer down and increase the price
without prior warning.

16. So don't delay any further: (Click Here To Get Instant Access To The Course Now. You won't Regret It.)

If you have any questions regarding this course, then feel free to get in touch with us at [Email]

Please Note: Even though this is a sketch work I bet it will convert when you do a little touch-up to it.

After you must have finished your sales letter, save and close your work, go and rest to calm your brain and on the next day when you're already refreshed come back and make changes and corrections. Don't make the mistake of trying to draft, correct, and publish your sales letter in one day to avoid unnecessary errors.

SUMMARY OF HOW TO WRITE A SALES LETTER

1.   write your headline

2.   Insert a video if you can

3.   Write the bullet points

4.   Enter a call-to-action

5.   Add social proof/testimonials

6.   State the problem

7.   Agitate the problem

8.   Back it up with facts

9.   Provide your solution

10. Describe the solution in detail

11. Back the solution with proof

12. Make an offer

13. Throw in some bonuses

14. State your price

15. Give a guarantee

16. Restate your offer

17. Close and add a call-to-action

18. Add a postscript

Note: The above examples are not live copies as the products used are not real products. They're just samples or temples to help you comprehend better.

Module 7

How To Write High-Converting Emails

According to Litmus and the Direct Marketing Association (they're one of the top and trusted marketing authorities in the whole world), for every $1 you spend on email marketing, you get back $48, which is a return on investment of 4800%. Trust me no other marketing strategy does this. According to research, email marketing has a conversion rate of 23%, which is better than social media which converts at 1%. So, it is safe to say that email marketing is the best way of building customer relationships and making sales.

Why Does Email Marketing Work So Well?

·   It doesn't cost a lot to implement

·   People may buy from you after multiple contact with them and not just the first time, unlike other marketing platforms.

The Problem With Email Marketing

·   Only a few percent of emails get opened

·   Only a few percentages of opened emails get read

·   Only a few percentage reads are acted upon

Tips For Writing Converting Emails

·   The sole objective of your email is to sell the click

·   Every email should have 3 parts: the subject line, the body, and the call-to-action.

·   Keep your emails as short as possible

· Each email should focus on one angle or theme.

· Bring your call-to-action to the top

What Are These Angles or Themes?

They are:

· Product benefits

· User testimonials

· Social proofs

· FAQ

· Satisfaction guarantees

· Unique selling proposition

· Bring your call-to-action to the top

A Good Subject Line

· A good subject line should Inspire curiosity

1. Read This If You Don't Want To Develop Heart Disease

2. 3 Weight Loss Lies You Believe

3. Here's Why The Government Don't Want You To Be Healthy

4. 3 Ways the Big Pharma Are Making You Sick

· Make the body relevant to the subject line

· Should be benefit-based: don't mistake features for benefits

· Use numerals instead of words

· Ask questions in your subject line

· Highlight recent news in your subject line: Breaking News…

· Keep your subject line under 50 characters (the shorter, the better)

· Use 3 or more of the above to write good email subject lines

HOW TO WRITE THE BODY OF YOUR EMAIL

· Maintain the flow from the subject line

· Keep sentences short

· Maintain a lot of white spaces (spaces with nothing written on them)

· Remove every word that your email can do without

THE CLOSING PART OF THE EMAIL

· The Call-To-Action

· Postscript (PS) [it's not really necessary]

HOW TO AVOID THE SPAM FOLDER

· Ask recipients to whitelist your email address

· Make your subscribers reply to your first email

· Avoid spam trigger words

DIFFERENT CATEGORIES OF EMAILS

1.   Stand-alone emails

2.   Sequential emails

1.   Stand Alone Emails:

They're sent to subscribers once they subscribe to your email list. They're sometimes called newsletters and they're not scheduled.

2.   Email Sequence:

They're a series of emails that are sent automatically as each email in the series is written to build upon the previous one. Once the emails are written and set up in an email service provider, they're sent at predetermined intervals or when someone takes a certain action. It is sometimes called Autoresponders, it can contain 3, 5, 7, 10, or more emails. The advantage of a sequence is unlike a newsletter, your recipients will receive your emails at the exact time they need to see them

TYPES OF EMAIL SEQUENCES

1.   Nurture or induction sequence

2.   Promotional sequence

3.   Onboarding sequence

4.   Cart abandonment sequence

5.   Reengagement sequence

1.   Nurture or Induction Sequence:

Introduces subscribers to your business and builds relationships with them (sent when a subscriber joins your email list). Also note: If you promised your subscribers any bonuses or eBook (lead magnet) when they joined your mailing list, the first email is where you fulfil that promise, you will also ask them to whitelist your email. Then set their expectations by letting them know the frequency and the content of the subsequent emails.

2.   Promotional Sequence:

They're used to pitch your products & services to your subscribers usually sent after the induction sequence.

3.   Onboarding Sequence:

They're used to welcome customers and also to make sure that they understand how to use the product or service.

4.   Cart Abandonment Sequence:

They're used on people who left an order without buying.

5.   Re-Engagement Sequence:

They're used to reestablish relationships with subscribers who have stopped opening or engaging with your emails or products.

Nurture or Induction Sequence

Examples:

Email 1

Subject line first:

Congrats [Enter First Name], Your Download is Inside

Hey [First Name],

It's [your name] here from **[ADULT FAT SHRINKER.com]**

I'm sending you this email because you entered your email on my website to receive my free report **(name what you're giving out).**

Now, I'm going to:

Give you access to the weight loss report

Show you how you can get access to my other weight loss resources.

So, let's get started

How to get the report you requested

This free report is called Shrinker's Guide **[name of your freebie]**

It contains closely guarded secrets that can help you get your dream body in the next couple of weeks.

So, **<u>Click Here To Download Your Copy.</u>**

Don't miss any important emails from me!

I'm going to be sending you a lot of weight-loss tips over the next few days.

But sometimes, the email client you use can make mistakes and filter my messages to your spam folder

If that happens, you will miss out on Important tips and updates

And who knows if that particular email you'll miss would have been the answer to your weight loss problems?

To prevent this from happening, all you have to do is whitelist my email

Click Here To Find Out How To Whitelist My Email *[add a link to a video of how to whitelist emails]*

Look out for my next email.

I'll send you an important message tomorrow in the email, I'll be talking about how I lost up to 28 lbs in 2 weeks

I did this without dieting or going to the gym

I'll tell you how you can do the same

Plus, I'll reveal some weight loss tips I'm sure you'll love

The email's subject line will be "How I Lost 60 lbs In 30 Days."

So make sure you read it when it arrives

Thanks, and have an awesome day.

[Your Name].

PS: Were you able to download the free guide?

If YES, reply to this email with "YES, I got the guide."

And if NO, reply with "NO, I couldn't get the guide," so I can send it as an attachment here.

Email 2

How I Lost 60 Lbs In 30 Days

Hey [First Name],

It's [your name] again

I want to congratulate you once again for joining my newsletter, where I teach people how to lose weight

Before I go on, I'd love to tell you about my weight-loss journey.

You see, I haven't always had the sexy lean body I have now

Instead, there was a time when I was in your shoes, struggling with excess body fat

Despite trying different supplements and diet plans, I was still seeing no positive results.

This not only affected my health, but it took a toll on my self-confidence too

You see, I have always been someone who would set goals and achieve them.

So, when I just couldn't achieve my weight loss goals, I stopped believing in myself

I also felt guilty that I couldn't wear the sexy clothes I wanted.

And I felt ashamed of my bulging stomach

In fact, people laughed at me and called me all sorts of names.

Things continued like this until one day, I made up my mind to give up.

That day, I looked at the time and money I was spending on different programs without getting any results and felt like a fool.

Then I told myself that I was going to quit trying so that I wouldn't waste any more time and money.

But the following day, something remarkable happened.

I took a public bus.

And the passenger beside me blurted out...

"You look so fat and ugly. And this seat is too small for you."

Everybody on the bus laughed and made fun of me and I felt ashamed.

But then I promised myself that I was going to do anything possible to lose weight.

Because that's the only way to prevent that kind of thing from happening to me again.

So, I went back and started researching and talking to weight-loss experts.

I bought every weight-loss product I saw online

Most of them didn't work, though.

In fact, nothing worked.

Until I discovered some hidden strategies that nobody had ever told me about before.

With these strategies, I made little but consistent progress.

Slowly but surely, I lost some weight

I will never forget how I managed to lose 60 lbs in one month with these strategies.

And that was how I got the sexy, lean body I have now.

Would you like to learn more about some strategies that worked for me?

I wrote a blog post about them

<u>Go Here To Check The Post Out Now If You Want To Lose Weight Naturally.</u>

Regards,

[Your Name]

Email 3:

3 Weight Loss Lies You Probably Believe

Hi Sam,

Did you know that most of the things weight loss gurus teach are lies?

Yes.

They feed you with lies so that you'll never lose weight

Do you know why they do that?

Because if you lose weight, you will stop buying their products

And since the only way they make money is to sell you products, they'll tell you lies to ensure you don't lose weight

I'm sick and tired of seeing them deceive innocent people

So, I have decided to expose their lies and reveal the truth to you.

Lies 1:

Lies 2:

Lies 3:

There you go.

The above lies are not just malicious but destructive too if you consider the side effects of those drugs on the body

There are many other things to expose.

And I believe that it will shatter some of your most closely held weight loss myths.

You'll feel weird and angry after reading it.

But I can't allow you to stay in the dark any longer.

So, I'm going to give you the link to an article that exposed a good number of their ugly lies so you'll read it yourself.

<u>Go Check Out The Article Here</u>

All the best,

[Name]

Or

10 Ugly Weight Loss Lies You Fall For!

Hi [Name],

Truth is…

A whole host of big ugly weight loss lies have been running free

Lies that you might even believe

In fact, the entire weight loss industry is built on a foundation of lies.

Not only are most of the products in the market today ineffective, they're downright dangerous.

For example, did you know weight loss pills are risky?

Neither did I!

But I just discovered that since they speed up metabolism, they can lead to high blood pressure and heart problems.

On top of that, most of the things weight loss gurus teach are wrong.

Things like…

High-fat diets will make you gain weight.

Low-fat diets are the key to burning fat quickly

Fasting will make you lose weight!

Exercise and visiting the gym every day are the keys to being skinny.

You need to work out a lot more to lose weight.

Literally, every one of those statements is dead wrong.

It's shocking, isn't it?

Luckily, I've found a short that revealed the truth.

According to the article, starvation makes the body go into survival mode, a situation that arises when one consumes too few calories.

In this situation, the body receives the message that it needs to protect itself.

This means holding onto weight for protection's sake.

What about over-exercising?

It stresses the body and causes the production of a protein called betatrophin.

Plus, your body will produce stress hormones like cortisol and adrenaline.

Betatrophin brings critical fat-burning enzymes to a complete standstill.

While the stress hormones will slow down the rate at which the body burns calories.

As for low-fat diets, they don't work because the body needs fats and proteins to activate some detoxifying and fat-burning enzymes.

So, when you eat too little fat, you'll notice a weight loss resistance.

There are many other things this article exposed.

So, I believe that it will shatter some of your most closely held weight-loss myths.

You'll feel weird and angry after reading it.

But I can't allow you to stay in the dark any longer.

So, I'm going to give you the link to the article, so you can read it yourself.

Go Check Out The Article Here

All the best,

[Name]

Email 4:

3 Natural Ways To Lose Weight

Hey [Name],

Yesterday, I exposed some of the lies and myths that exist in the weight loss industry.

Today, I'm going to share my top tips for losing weight fast.

I figured most of these strategies out through trial and error.

They worked for me when I was trying to lose weight

And that's why I strongly believe that they will work for you too.

So, make sure you read this entire email.

I decided to focus on these 3 tips alone because they're simple and easy to implement

Most importantly, they can help you to start seeing weight loss results right away

Excited?

Let's get right down to the strategies:

Strategy 1

Strategy 2

Strategy 3

That's it!

Implementing these strategies alone could help you to lose 7 lbs in 1 week.

But if you're looking for even faster ways to achieve your weight loss goals naturally, you need to check my next email.

In that email, I'll share more weight loss strategies you can use to lose up to 2 lbs every day.

Talk soon

[Your Name]

Email 5:

Gifts From My Treasury To You

Hi [Name],

In my last email, I shared 3 of my top weight-loss strategies

Now, I'm going to talk about 2 other crazy strategies

These 2 strategies are even more powerful than those I gave you last time

Yet they go unnoticed by the overwhelming majority of people.

If you've been searching for effective weight loss strategies for some time but haven't come across one yet…

…Don't beat yourself up too much.

Although they seem simple, they're still elusive, and even some weight-loss coaches don't know how effective they are.

This means that once you start using them, you will have an unfair advantage over the majority of people trying to lose weight.

Ready to find out what they are?

I'm talking about **[mention the unique strategy 4 and 5]**

[Talk about strategy 4]

[Talk about strategy 5]

Are you starting to see how powerful these strategies are?

If you put them into practice, you'll be amazed at the kind of results they will give you.

Hopefully, you've found this email helpful.

But there are still more gifts from my treasury you probably don't know about that could be the answer to your weight loss problem.

It's the most powerful natural weight-loss strategy I have ever seen.

And I'd even go so far as to say that if you're not using it, you are definitely holding yourself back.

Luckily, we will cover it in detail in my next email.

So be on the lookout for it.

Cheers,

[Your Name]

Email 6

Unveiled: The Most Powerful Strategy So Far!

Hi [Name],

Let's pick up right where we left off in my last email

The weight loss strategy we are going to unveil today is **[strategy 6]**

This is by far the most powerful strategy you could add to your weight-loss arsenal

I'll explain in a second

But first, let me explain what **[strategy 6]** is

[Full explanation of strategy 6]

So, you see how powerful this strategy is

If you combine it with the other tips and strategies I gave you in my previous emails…

…you will not only lose weight faster but also keep it forever

So, go and apply the tips and strategies starting today, and don't just forget to keep me posted with your questions and results.

Regards,

[Your Name].

Email 7

The Hardest Thing About Losing Weight

Hi [name],

One of the hardest parts of trying to lose weight is knowing exactly what works and what doesn't

You have to solve problems on your own the majority of the time.

The kind of exercise that works

The type of weight-loss supplement that's safe

The types of workout plans and diet plans that are effective and the ones that are not

And you have to rely on the internet to help you with all these

The problem!

For every bit of good content, you see online, there are 10 pieces of junk

You can't 100% trust any advice you get

And you won't have any idea if something will work until you try it out for yourself

Curious if this diet plan will work?

You have to try it and find out.

Will the other workout plan work?

Go ahead and try it with crossed fingers.

Wondering if the new supplement works?

Buy and try one month's supply of it.

It won't have any negative side effects, hopefully.

And what if you find something that works?

What if you want to share it with other weight-loss experts and get their feedback?

There's no good way to do that

Because those experts won't try the strategy to verify that it works.

So, I had an idea

It's a blog, Facebook group, or YouTube Channel for you, me, and everyone else looking to lose weight

You can check it out here…

In this blog, group, and channel, I'll be sharing my best weight loss tips and secrets.

I'm talking about the strategies that have been tested and proven to be effective by me and a lot of others

You'll be able to share your own weight-loss journey and discoveries too.

Plus, whenever you're stuck, you can ask questions and get answers instantly.

More importantly, you'll be able to interact with like-minded people.

My students who have achieved their weight-loss goals are sharing what worked for them there.

You're going to like this channel, group, or blog.

<u>So Click Here To Check It Out Now!</u>

Regards,

[Your Name].

HOW TO WRITE A PROMOTIONAL EMAIL SEQUENCE

We will write this from these angles

- Value angle

- PAS angle

- Testimonial angle

- Benefit angle

- USP (unique selling proposition/point) angle

- Story-based angle

- FAQ angle

- Closing angle

PROMOTIONAL EMAIL SEQUENCE

Examples:

Email 1: Value Angle

Here's Your Download: [first name]

Hey [first name],

I prefer to deliver upon my promises more than anything else

So as promised, **Click Here To Download your copy Of [name of your lead magnet]**

I also told you that I was going to show you simple ways to lose weight

So here are 10 of them:

1.   Eat breakfast every day

        If you skip breakfast because you want to cut calories, you'll end up eating more throughout the day.

2.   Close the kitchen at night.

        This way, you won't give in to the late-night munchies or mindless snacking.

3.   Reduce your intake of sweetened drinks.

        They pile on the calories but don't reduce hunger like solid foods do.

4.   Eat more fruits and vegetables.

        They crowd out other foods that are higher in fat and calories.

5.   Substitute whole grains for refined grains.

        This way, you'll fill up faster and be more likely to eat a reasonable portion.

6.   Take charge of your surroundings; this includes everything from choosing the best eateries to loading your kitchen with nutritious options.

7.   Trim portions. Try reducing it by 10%–20%.

8.   Get more active. You can pace while you talk on the phone, take the dog out for an extra walk, and march in place during television commercials

9.   Have protein at every meal and snack. You'll be less prone to overeat because of this extended sensation of fullness.

10. Switch to the low-fat versions of salad dressings, mayonnaise, dairy products, and other products.

There you have it.

10 simple, painless strategies to help you lose weight without going on a diet.

What to expect next!

I want to make sure that you achieve your weight loss goals FAST

So, over the next few days, I will share more tips to help you burn fat and get your dream body.

Tips that have worked for hundreds of people in your situation.

I'm sure you're going to love what I have in store for you.

But if not, it's really simple to unsubscribe by clicking on the link at the bottom of my emails.

And I promise there will be no hard feelings :)

What Should You Do Next?

If you don't want to risk missing out, then you should add my email address to your contact list right now.

This will ensure that all my emails make it to your inbox in the future.

Regards,

[Your name]

Email 2: Use the PAS angle.

Giving Up Is Not An Option: See Why

[First name],

Since you're on this email list, I know you're struggling with excess body fat.

You've spent a lot of time trying to solve this problem

Even worse, you've wasted a lot of money on different weight-loss products

I know, I've been there

And it's terrible

Being overweight can make your whole life miserable

It can prevent you from wearing those clothes you admire because they won't fit you.

It can drain your energy, and you end up panting over little tasks.

And it can prevent you from feeling comfortable, attractive, and confident.

Worse of all, it will put you at risk of heart disease and other serious health issues.

But the good news is that it's not hard to lose weight

In fact, with just a few minor changes in your daily habits, you could burn off 60 lbs in a month.

I have done it before

I have helped hundreds of people in your situation to do it too.

And for the first time, I have compiled all the strategies that worked for me and those people into a simple guide

This guide is called **"ADULT FAT SHRINKER"** weight loss guide

And with the strategies inside this guide, many of my students were able to burn 2 lbs every day.

That's 14 lbs a week and 60 lbs a month.

If you want to achieve similar results, click the link below to get this guide today

<u>**Go Here To Check Out the "ADULT FAT SHRINKER" Weight Loss Guide.**</u>

I look forward to helping you get the body of your dreams

[Your Name]

Email 3: Benefit Angle

You Ought To Have Known This

Hi [first name],

In my last email, I told you about my **"ADULT FAT SHRINKER"** weight loss guide.

However, I forgot to tell you the benefits that the guide will help you achieve

You see, the secrets and strategies in that guide didn't just help people lose weight…

But it also helped them to:

Boost their immune system and decrease the risk of diseases

Combat tiredness and fatigue

Achieve optimum mental and physical performance

Get the kind of lean body they're always proud to show off

Skyrocket their energy level and focus

Begin to feel you are beautiful again

Take their confidence and productivity to a higher level

Combat the effects of rapid aging and look and feel 10 years younger

Begin to look better, feel better, and sleep better.

To me, these are some of the benefits you ought to have known about losing weight

My **"ADULT FAT SHRINKER"** weight-loss guide will help you to achieve all of the above and more

Best of all, you can get the guide today at 70% off the real price

<u>Click Here To Find Out More About The Guide And Get Your Copy Today.</u>

Cheers,

[Your Name]

Email 4: USP or Unique Selling Point Angle

This Is Not A "Me-Too" Guide – See It For Yourself

 Or

It's Unlike What You've Seen Before

[First Name],

Yesterday, I told you about my weight loss guide and how you can get a copy of it

I also told you that this guide has helped a lot of people to lose up to 60 lbs in one month

But you still haven't gotten your copy of it

I see just one possible explanation for this:

You're probably thinking that this guide is like the ones you've seen before…

…those that didn't give you any result

There are a ton of weight loss classes that teach people how to lose weight, you could even be thinking.

After all, I've seen most of them, if not all.

The difference, however, is that my guide blew all of the others out of the water

It's not one of those thrashy PDF reports that regurgitate the same old information you've heard before

NO!

It's the most comprehensive and up-to-date resource on how to lose weight naturally.

Everything you'll learn from it is backed by years of experience, research, and testing.

Inside, you will find **XX** Chapters that are set up in a progressive learning format.

Most weight loss eBooks I've seen in the past are confusing and full of boring theories

That's why I broke up this one into different chapters to make things a lot easier for people to learn and implement.

Everything is simplified and laid out for you step-by-step, so there's no more guesswork.

On top of that, I won't just give you a guide and leave you to go and implement everything alone.

Instead, I'll offer you personalized coaching to guide you to your weight loss goals.

If that sounds like something you'd like, then **Click Here To Get This Guide Today.**

Regards,

[Your Name]

Email 5: Use Testimonial Angle.

What John & My Other Students Are Saying

Hey [first name],

Since the first day I mentioned my **"ADULT FAT SHRINKER"** weight loss guide, lots of people have been asking to see proof that it works.

They want to be sure that the secrets and strategies in this guide will really help them lose weight and get their dream body

I perfectly understand

After all, it's easy for anyone to claim that their guide is the best in the world

However, the real proof is in the results people are getting with the guide

Right?

That's why instead of saying "Trust Me", I rather show you what others are saying after they bought the guide and put it to use

First here is an update from **[John]**. He wrote this about the guide:

[Insert John's testimonial]

For Marian, here's what she said about the guide:

[Insert Maria's testimonial]

Wood Mark says this too:

[Insert Wood's testimonial]

That's not all though

There are more great comments, reviews, and testimonials from other people who have gone through this awesome guide.

However, posting all of them here will make this email long and really boring.

<u>You Can See A Lot More Here, Including Videos To Show They Are Real</u>

The bottom line is:

These testimonials are proof that the secrets and strategies in this guide work

And it has helped hundreds of people in your situation to achieve their weight loss goals

So, if you want to achieve similar or even better results than those you saw in these testimonials…

...Then Click Here To Find Out More About It And Get A Copy Of This Guide Today - you won't regret it.

Cheers,

[Your Name]

Email 6: Use FAQ Angle

Are These Questions Going On In Your Head?

Hey [first name],

I get asked many questions about my **"ADULT FAT SHRINKER"** weight loss guide

So today, I'm going to do a bit of **"Q n A"**

In this case, if you have these questions in your head, then you'll get the answers right here.

Question 1: What's this guide about?

It's a comprehensive course created to help people like you lose weight, transform their bodies, and begin to love themselves again.

It's like having a certified weight loss coach work with you personally until you achieve your weight loss goals.

And that's why it has helped many people like you get the body of their dreams.

Question 2: Who created this guide?

I'm a certified weight loss and fitness coach specialist who has helped hundreds of people struggling to lose weight.

I created this guide based on what worked for me and the hundreds of individuals I've worked with.

Question 3: What will I get when I order?

You'll get access to:

A PDF eBook containing all the most effective weight-loss techniques

A community of like-minded people who have benefited from the training. These are people you'll learn from their experiences and who will cheer you to success

personalized coaching where I'll connect one-on-one with you periodically to listen to your weight loss problems and offer you individualized advice.

XX powerful bonuses that will help you accelerate your results.

Unlimited support whenever you need help

And so much more!

<u>Click Here To Find Out How To Get This Guide Now!</u>

Question 4: Everything about this guide sounds good. How much will it cost me?

Unlike some weight loss products that cost a fortune, this particular guide was created not for me to make money but to help people like you get the body of their dreams.

That's why all you have to pay to get this guide is **$XX**

Question 5: Is this not too expensive?

Look, if you were to pay separately for everything that comes with this guide, you would end up spending not less than **XX**.

In fact, that's the actual value of the guide.

So, paying **$XX** for it is actually dirt cheap.

Question 6: Are there any other fees for me to pay?

No. There are no hidden charges or upsells. All you have to pay is the one-time fee of **$XX.**

Question 7: I have gone through similar guides before, but they didn't work for me. How can I be positive it will?

If you've been disappointed by other weight loss programs you've bought before, there's only one reason for that: none of them come with personalized coaching. So, you end up following strategies that may work for other people but not for your particular situation.

However, my guide is different. You won't just get a PDF guide, but the opportunity to be coached by me. The reviews, success stories, and testimonials on this page are proof that the strategies you'll learn from the guide work!

Question 8: What if I don't like the guide?

This guide has helped a lot of people to achieve their weight loss goals…Other weight-loss experts have confirmed that my guide is top-notch. That's why I'm 100% sure that it can help you too.

However, if, after going through the guide and implementing the strategies therein, you think it's short of your expectations, then I'll refund you.

Question 9: Do you provide support when one buys the guide?

Yes, with my guide, you won't have to do it alone. That's because help is just an email away, no matter the issue you're facing. You'll also get 24/7 support via email, private chat, or our closed Facebook group.

Question 10: I want to order right away. How can I get instant access?

<u>Simply Click Here To Get A Copy Of The Guide.</u>

You'll be grateful to me for years to come, I assure you.

Question 11: I have other questions that aren't listed here.

If you have more questions, then **<u>Visit This Page And Scroll To The Bottom Where You'll Find My Comprehensive FAQ Section.</u>**

Better still, you can reply to this email with your question, and I'll get back to you with the answers in 24 hours or less.

Regards,

[Name].

Email 7: Closing email (here introduces Fear of Missing Out FOMO).

Last Chance!

Hey [first name],

I've been sending you emails to tell you about my awesome weight loss guide…

…and how it can help you lose up to 60 lbs in just one month.

Did you see the emails?

Well, frankly speaking, I'm still mystified because you haven't gotten a copy yet…

…even though you've seen proof that it's really helping others in your situation.

That's why I decided to take a minute to write and let you know that I'm planning to close the sales of this guide by 11:59 p.m. today.

I may stop selling earlier if the few remaining copies I have get taken before 11:59 p.m.

The reason I'm doing this is to limit the number of people who have access to this guide.

That way, I'll be able to give one-on-one support to everybody.

So, if you read this email tomorrow, then I apologize because it will be too late.

If you decide to get the guide, then you may not be able to do so.

And you may have to wait until I start selling again, which may be next year

Or you'll miss the opportunity to use my proven-to-work strategies to achieve your weight loss goals.

<u>So Click Here To Find Out More And Get Your Copy Of This Guide Now Before I Close The Sales By 11:59 pm</u>

Good Luck!

[Your Name].

SUMMARY OF HOW TO WRITE A GREAT EMAIL

· The sole objective of your email is to sell the click

· Every email should have 3 parts

· Keep your emails as short as possible

· One email, one angle

· Bring your call-to-action to the top

· A good subject line should inspire curiosity

· A good subject line should be benefit-based

· Use numerals instead of words

· Ask questions in your subject lines

· Highlight recent news in your subject line

· Keep your subject lines under 50 characters

·   Maintain the flow from the subject line in the body

·   Keep sentences short

·   Maintain lots of white spaces

·   Remove every word that your email can do without

·   Ask your recipients to whitelist your email address

·   Make your subscribers reply to your first email.

Note: The above examples are not live copies, as the products used are not real products. They're just samples or temples to help you comprehend better.

Module 8:

How To Write High-Converting Video Sales Letter (VSL)

It is using engaging, attention-grabbing, and high-converting videos to sell your products or services. Video sales Letters Convert Better Than Text Sales Letters. Video marketing generates more sales than every other form of marketing.

Video landing pages improve conversions by at least 80%, according to wordstream.com.

This means that putting a sale video on your page doubles your sales conversion.

This is because, statistically speaking, 80% of people prefer videos over written text.

...72% of customers prefer watching videos to learn about new products and services.

Only 22% prefer reading articles, infographics, eBooks, and presentations.

...2 out of every 3 customers get purchase ideas from watching videos

...50% of online users search for product videos before they make a purchase.

While viewers retain 95% of a message when they watch it in a video, compared to 10% when reading it in text,

These are proven facts from companies like Sisco, Forbes, Google, etc. But why do videos convert better?

Videos convert better because they combine visual imagery, sound, special effects, and text headings that offer people a rich picture of what is being communicated. Let's write a sample of a VSL.

TIPS TO WRITING A HIGH-CONVERTING VSL

Give room for breathing (so that it can look conversational)

Your VSL must start with an attention-grabbing headline

Example:

Start with an attention-grabbing headline.

Pay Attention To This Video If You're Experiencing Difficulty Losing Weight.

Are you going to let excess body fat ruin your life?

Even though many people will tell you that there's nothing wrong with being overweight...

...it can make your whole life miserable

Because you're overweight:

You'll stop wearing the clothes you love because they won't fit.

You'll no longer feel comfortable, attractive, or confident in your body

You'll start to look ugly, unfit and unhealthy

143

You won't have the stamina to complete tasks.

And people will start laughing at you and calling you names.

Here: agitate the problem as in your sales letter.

However, that's just the start of your issue.

You could also lose your partner

Or, are you wondering how that's possible?

Okay, I'll tell you

First, let me ask you this:

Do you know the number-one reason men cheat?

Especially married men and those in serious relationships

The reason is that they no longer find their partner attractive

Men want to be with ladies who are lean, fit, and beautiful

And when a woman becomes fat and ugly, her man will look for another attractive lady

As you are watching this video, there are chances that your man is cheating with your neighbor

Even if he still tells you that you're attractive, he may have replaced you in his heart

Worst of all, being overweight can lead to fatty materials building up in your arteries

Additionally, a heart attack may result from damage and blockage to the arteries that provide blood to the heart.

It can also lead to other serious heart diseases that cause early death

So right now, you're at risk of heart disease and early death

Here: add social proof.

It's not necessary for you to be too hard on yourself.

After all, it's not your fault and you are not alone

You see, over 70% of US adults are overweight

And just like you, millions more all over the world

And the number keeps increasing every day

This is why the weight-loss industry is a multibillion-dollar industry

Together with the big pharma, it keeps bringing out expensive and ineffective solutions

They make billions from selling their useless supplement and weight-loss pills to you

I mean pills that have dangerous side effects

Now, if you keep buying these products, you'll not only be wasting money...

...but you'll also be putting your health on the line

Here bring in the solution.

Fortunately for you, there's a brand-new solution

Something that's guaranteed to help you lose 60 lbs in just one month

It's natural, and there's no side effect to using it

It doesn't also require that you go on strict dieting, starve yourself, or avoid foods that you love

Neither does it require painful and expensive surgeries

It doesn't even require that you go to the gym or engage in hard-to-do exercises

Here, before you reveal the solution, build suspense and scarcity to keep your audience glued.

I'll reveal this solution to you shortly

But first, I need to warn you

This video may not be available for a long time

So, make sure you drop everything you're doing right now and watch it to the end

You see, what I'm about to reveal is highly controversial

To be blunt, this stuff could be devastating to the medical and pharmaceutical industry

They're aware of the natural and effective weight loss strategies that I'm about to reveal

But if people like you get to know it, they will lose billions

So, whenever they see videos like this, they'll fight with everything they have to bring it down

They will go as far as paying Google to prevent this video from showing up on search engines

And they can even bribe my web hosting company to shut down my website

Honestly, I can't predict what they're going to do next...or what lengths they will go to remove this video

So, all I ask is that you watch it to the end while it's still available

Here: provide proof. You have made your audience a big promise of providing a solution to their problem.

To prove to you that what I'm about to reveal works…

...let me show you people who have used it to achieve their weight loss goals

Anabel used it to lose 30 lbs in 2 weeks

Joyce used it to go from 120 lbs to 60 lbs in one month

Augusta used it to get back in shape before her wedding

In the above, read-out testimonials are not good enough, you should get pictures or video testimonials of the customers who have used your product or service. It will make your proof believable.

The next thing is to show your authority, you can do this by introducing yourself, your credentials, and what you do. (It is called expert positioning). You have to position yourself as an expert so that your audience will take you seriously.

Now, let me ask you

Would you like to achieve similar or even better results?

I'll show you how my brand-new solution will help you do that

My name is [your name]

And I'm a certified weight loss expert

But 5 years ago, I found myself in your shoes, struggling to lose weight

I tried different diets, supplements, and workout plans

But none of them gave me the results I wanted

I was on the verge of giving up on my weight loss goals, but something inside me told me to try harder

So, I started reading and asking questions

I also started researching, using all the resources at my disposal

I was determined to find a solution to my weight loss problems

During my research, I tested every weight loss formula I came across

I also experimented with all the natural and synthetic fat-burning substances I heard about

As I did research, I would write down what worked and what didn't work

At the end of the research, I found out that I had lost about 60 lbs

And I did it without strict dieting, going to the gym, or taking expensive and dangerous weight loss pills

Then I went to the book I recorded everything and found out that only a few of the formulas actually worked

So, I took those ones that worked and gave them to other people to try.

The result shocked me

All these people were able to lose weight and slim down to their ideal size

Yes

A 100% success rate

And that's why I'm sure that those formulas will work for anybody, including you

Here if you have any awards with your expertise, you add them.

Then it's time to give them the solution, but don't just give them the name, also add the features and benefits of your product or service. And make sure you don't give away too much information.

Now, I have compiled all the formulas into an easy-to-understand guide

And the good news is that I'm about to hand over the guide to you

That way, you will be able to lose weight and start enjoying the level of happiness that I enjoy now

I am introducing you to my **"ADULT FAT SHRINKER" weight loss guide**

This guide will show you natural ways to burn fat – without dieting or going to the gym

You'll be able to get your dream body.

You'll become healthy, fit, and attractive once again.

You'll regain your self-confidence and your energy.

And you'll say goodbye to the embarrassment and shame you go through when people laugh at you.

Here are some of the things you'll discover from the guide:

[List of everything they will learn inside the guide]

Imagine losing 60 lbs in just one month

Imagine getting the sexy bikini body of top celebrities

Imagine boosting your immune system and reducing your risk of diseases

Imagine combating constant tiredness and fatigue

Imagine skyrocketing your productivity and confidence to their highest levels

Imagine turning heads around everywhere you go

Imagine feeling attractive, sexy, and beautiful again

Imagine the excitement you'll get when your family and friends ask you… "How's it possible for you to look like this? Your body looks amazing! What did you do?

All these and more are the results you will experience if you get your hands on this guide today.

At this point show them more proof that it works. Remember the more testimonials you have the better for you.

Still Skeptical?

Okay, take a look at what other people are saying about this guide

[Insert pictures or video testimonials]

So, you see, the secrets in this guide work

It's really like a switch you need to flip, to get the kind of body you desire.

At this point add your offer: remember that an offer is everything the customer gets when he/she buys your product/services. A good offer is always a combination of the main product, discounted price, and bonuses.

Now, I'm sure you are eager to know how to get your hands on this guide

Right?

Okay, relax, I'll show you in just a second

However, allow me to ask you a quick question first.

How much would you pay right now to get your dream body?

Would you pay a hundred dollars? $200, $300, or even $1,000?

You see when I was in your shoes, I was ready to give my whole savings to it

Or who wouldn't want to pay any amount to save himself or herself from the risk of heart disease and early death that comes with excessive body fat?

In fact, anything that can help you lose weight is a lifesaver

And it's priceless

Looking at that, I can ask you to pay $250 for this guide and not feel guilty.

After all, most other people charge more than that for solutions that don't even work.

But I'm not selling this guide to become rich.

I have a business that makes me 8 figures.

So, I created this guide just to help people.

I had even thought of giving it away 100% free.

But the reason I later changed my mind is that I paid my webmaster to host this website.

And I don't want to be taking money out of my own pocket to make that monthly payment.

So, I have to charge a little money to cover the hosting and other expenses.

That's why I'm charging just **$XX** for this guide.

I'm serious.

All you need is less than **$XX** to get a copy of this guide.

This online payment will not only give you access to the guide, but you will also get **XX** bonuses valued at **$XX**.

These bonuses include:

[Mention the bonuses.]

The next thing is to make them take the offer immediately. Create scarcity. Like offering limited-time bonuses, or that the price will increase and always stating the reason for the scarcity. If you can always use a countdown timer to indicate the time remaining, most importantly, whenever you create scarcity, stick to it. It gives you more credibility.

But wait!

You have to hurry

This is because the **$XX** discount price won't be available for long

I'm planning to increase the price of the guide in the next **XX** days

And that's because, as much as I want to help people, I still want to benefit from my work.

Remember that I spent a lot of time, money, and other resources to research and create this guide

So, for the next **XX** days, you can ethically steal my **"ADULT FAT SHRINKER"** weight loss guide for just **$XX**

After that, the price goes up to **$XX**

At least at that price, I'd be able to make some money to compensate for my hard work

The last element to add is the guarantee: people are afraid of losing their money if the product doesn't work out for them.

Now, I know you're skeptical

You're asking yourself: What if this doesn't work for me?

You're scared that you may lose the **$XX** you paid for it

And I know why

You've probably been scammed

You've seen many other weight-loss guides out there

You've seen other solutions

And you've tried them

But you were disappointed

Well, I tried dozens of them too

And they all disappointed me

So, I perfectly understand your skepticism

But don't worry, I'm going to remove all the risks from you

Let me explain

I know that my guide will help you lose weight

And for that reason, I want to invite you to try it out without obligation

So, here's what you should do:

Go ahead and get your own copy of this guide today

If, after 60 days of implementing the secrets inside, you didn't see any results...

...Let me know, and I'll refund you every cent you paid. No questions asked!

(Now close with a call to action.)

<u>Click The Button Below This Video Now To Order This Guide, So You Can Start Losing Weight.</u>

Note: Remember that it does not need to be this long. If this is a life copy, it will never be this lengthy, but for illustration purposes, it ended up this way. But if yours can be engaging, then it can be long too. Remember to practice each module.

The above examples are not live copies, as the products used are not real products. They're just samples or temples to help you comprehend better.

Module 9:

How To Write A Storytelling Copy

To get your audience to take action in any marketing copy, telling a good story is the way. There's nothing more engaging than a good story. Good stories help to tap into your audiences' emotions. And people don't buy products based on logic, no, they buy based on emotions. Stories inspire prospects to make purchases.

TIPS TO BECOMING A GREAT STORYTELLER

· Make your story personal

· Always start your story with a hook (a hook is a statement that will get people's attention and make them eager to know what happened next; here you begin at the middle of the story, this is because most beginnings are not as captivating as the middle)

· Ensure that it pertains to the item you are marketing.

· Your stories should be short

· Stick to what's important

· Structure it in a way that keeps your audience interested

· Show; don't just tell

·   Tell more stories

Structure Of A Good Story

1.   A beginning

2.   A conflict

3.   A climax

4.   And an end.

How To Create Your Hero's Journey

1.   The departure act represents the beginning of the story and is also the stage when the hero sets out to get his prize.

2.   The Initiation Act represents the middle of the story, and that is the stage where the hero encounters many conflicts and setbacks on the road to his price.

3.   The return act represents the end of the story. That's the stage when the hero returns home with his prize, transformed.

These 3 stages are divided into 12 steps, but I have compressed them into 8 steps to make it simpler for you.

STEPS TO CREATING YOUR HERO'S JOURNEY

1.   The ordinary world (this represents when your hero is still living an ordinary life before his quest began)

2.   The call to adventure (when the hero is faced with a challenge or a problem)

3.   Crossing the first threshold (this represents the point when the hero sets out on a journey to get the solution to the above problem or conflict)

4.   The roads of trials (at this stage the hero is faced with trials and setbacks and may even consider giving up on his journey at this point but after learning some lessons from his trials he makes up his mind to continue his quest).

5.   The approach (here the hero tries a new approach that is different from the one he's been trying before that didn't work).

6.   The reward (here the hero accomplishes his goal with the new approach)

7.   The road back (this is where the hero's life changes completely because of the goal he has achieved)

8.   The return with the elixir (here the hero uses the knowledge he has gained to help other people).

TYPES OF STORIES YOU CAN TELL IN YOUR COPY

·   Personal stories

·   Case studies

·   Stories that teach something

·   Examples

·   Future pacing

· Myths, Misconceptions And Mistakes

Story 1:

I won't forget the day I had a heart attack

As I was preparing for work that Friday morning, my heart began to wrench like a crinkled paper

As I stumbled to the floor, I tried to call for help

But I couldn't breathe, and I couldn't shout either

My mouth opened and closed repeatedly but no sound came out

And as I lay on the ground in an awkward position, not having the strength to even move at all…

…helpless but terrified, I realized I was having some sort of heart attack

A Personal Stories:

Template:

Just 3 years ago, I was overweight

Back then, I could not wear the sexy clothes I danced

On top of that, I was ashamed of my bulging stomach

People even laughed at me and called me all sorts of names...the worst of it being "Belleti"

When I couldn't take the embarrassment any longer, I decided that something had to be done

So, I went online and started searching for effective weight-loss products

But despite trying dozens of supplements, pills, and diet plans I found, I was still not seeing any positive result

So, I went back and started researching and talking to weight loss experts

I bought every weight loss product that was recommended to me and the ones I saw online, and nothing still worked

I was considering giving up when I stumbled on some secrets I had never heard of before

These secrets changed everything and worked almost from the first day I used it

So, I compiled these secrets into a simple guide for myself so I can easily follow it

In 30 days of using these secrets, I lost 60 lbs

And you know what?

The secrets have nothing to do with dieting or going to the gym

Right now, I have the sexy lean body I had always dreamed of

A Case Study:

Template:

A client of mine sent me this story:

Laboriously she makes her way from her house to the bus stop...

She is already at the bus stop stand, tired and even struggling to catch her breath when she subconsciously looks up.

At first, she didn't notice any awkwardness of the steers coming from bystanders… with a closer look she noticed the disgust in their eyes as they looked at her

It's as if she just shit herself

So, she unconsciously double-checked her body mentally at least to be sure…

In that confused state… skiiiiii!!! Wow the bus has arrived

And as she's trying to hop on the bus of course with difficulty

The driver just said, "We don't have the whole day fatso hurry and stop wasting our time..."

Previously, she was confused but now she's covered in shame

"Hahahahaha, I bet she could eat the whole Walmart if given the chance," says a passenger.

And the whole passengers erupted into loud deafening laughter

Oooh no, the door of the bus's shut… and she has no option but to slowly walk her way through the aisle to find a place to sit with her face down

As She made her way to an empty seat at the back, she could literally feel their eyes boring holes... into her soul,

suddenly her mind wanders off to that steer of disgust at the bus stand and now she could feel not just a steer of disgust but that of mockery as the laughter raged on

She's lost, she can't breathe, it's like her mind is shutting down, she starts feeling light-headed, oh no she can hear her heartbeat pound and it's pounding uncontrollably; her sight begins to blur and... oops

She wakes up in the hospital and the doctor tells her that she just had a cardiac arrest… she walks out of the hospital diagnosed with high blood pressure which was caused by cholesterol (excessive fat in the veins)

Well, this was Lycia 60 days ago, and there is a likelihood of you ending up in this exact situation or worse.

Maybe because of how liberal our society is today people or even relatives, friends, and your partner may not mock you publicly but they certainly feel disgusted on the inside trust me I have been there…

Or

 Take Lucy for example

She found my **"ADULT FAT SHRINKER"** weight loss tea when she was desperately looking to lose weight

According to her, she had been struggling with her weight since her teen

And after a few years, she figured that she had had enough

So, after trying lots of diets, supplements, pills, and workout programs that didn't work, she stumbled on our website

However, she looked at our supplements with a lot of skepticism

But the fact that we offered a 60–day money back guarantee made her decision a lot easier

...Because she figured that she had nothing to lose

So, she bought the supplement and started taking it as directed

Now, she sent us an email two days ago saying that the results she achieved were better than she thought would be possible for her

In the first week, she lost about 4–5 lbs

According to her, that was encouraging, but she still passed it off as circumstantial, thinking that next week she'd be back at her regular weight

Long story short, after one month, she had lost 30 lbs

And in another 30 days period, she had reached 58 lbs loss

It would be an understatement to say she was ecstatic.

Stories That Teach Something:

Sample:

People are not interested in you

They are not interested in the mission and vision of your business

Neither are they interested in the features of your products or services

What they're interested in is the benefits they will derive from them

So, when writing your sales copy, skip the features and list the benefits of what you want to sell

Or

Imagine this:

Mr. Chris went to a phone store to buy himself a phone

And immediately he walked in, a salesman met him and said:

Welcome to CNET Communications

Here, we sell all kinds of phones at affordable prices

Right now, we have a phone that is brand new in the market called the iPhone 30

It has the following features:

60,000mah battery, 25w charging support, 100-megapixel camera, and 1 TB memory

Now imagine that another salesperson comes to Mr Chris and says:

We have a new phone and I'm sure you'll like it

This phone can contain more than 50 thousand music files, 100 thousand pictures, and 10 thousand video files, and even limitless storage for document files

So, you can use it to save everything that's important to you

It can take very high-quality digital pictures so you can use it to capture and preserve the important moments of your life

And once you charge the phone, the battery can stay for one week under heavy usage

That means the phone won't go off while you're away from home, or when you're in the middle of some important discussion

And it takes only 20 minutes to charge the phone battery to full capacity

In this case, now, who do you think Mr. Chris will buy from?

The first salesperson or the second salesperson?

I'm sure he'll go for the second salesperson

And that's because benefits sell more than features

Stories By Examples:

Sample:

This is Paul

Just last month, he came to me for help because he was overweight

Then I recommended this organic detoxification and weight loss tea to him

Now, he is 45 lbs lighter?

How did he do it?

Well, it's simple.

Whenever he woke up in the morning, he would get a glass of clean water.

Then he would empty one sachet of this tea into the glass.

And finally, he would drink it before taking his breakfast.

That's it.

When I asked Paul what he liked most about the tea, he said:

"I liked the fact that I didn't have to go to the gym.

And I didn't have to change the kind of food I love eating to lose weight.

I like the taste too, it's delicious"

Future Pacing:

Sample:

Imagine for a moment that you lost 30 lbs in the next two weeks

You wake up in the morning, see your reflection in the bathroom mirror, and become overwhelmed with a sense of awe at how utterly stunning you look

There are no more wrinkles on your face, and so you look 15 years younger

You have more energy

You fit into your old tight jeans once again

You have the kind of sexy bikini body that attracts the opposite sex

And your partner starts loving you more than before

He starts treating you like the queen you are

And he's no more able to step out without taking you along…

...because he's now proud of you

He wants to show you off at all times

Now, imagine stepping into the office where you work

Everybody's attention is on you

And all your colleagues will be asking you:

"How's it possible that you look so amazing right now? How did you manage to shed off those fats?"

Imagine how excited you'll be to hear that

Imagine how your whole life will change just because you were able to shed off those excessive misery-bringing body fats

The 3 M's Of Content (Myths, Misconceptions and Mistakes).

Sample:

This reminds me of my cousin sister Jane

Jane is a time traveler

Seriously–she's always loving 30, 60, or even 90 days into the future

Whenever we talk, she tells me about the things she's going to buy once she loses weight

New high-heel shoes, tight jeans, and some bikini tops

She will then take a short vacation with her boyfriend

And wear bikinis while they build sand castles on the beach

This list of things Jane plans to do is virtually endless.

And she will only start them as soon as she has lost weight.

But the problem is…

She believes that low-calorie diets are the key to losing weight

This myth was handed down to her by one self-made weight loss guru she saw online

"If consuming fewer calories than I burn helps me lose fat, why can't severe calorie restriction provide even faster results?"

That's the question she always asked me whenever I tried to tell her the truth about diets and weight loss

And she held on to this misconception like a magnet.

Little did she know that when she went on a low-calorie diet, she began to starve herself.

And her body will think that she is stranded with no food.

As a result, her body's metabolism will slow down to prevent her from losing weight

I'm not sure how many times I've heard her say:

"This is the one low-calorie diet plan that will help me lose weight!"

But when I check back in a month, I always hear the same story…

"Oh, that one? It was not working for me, so I quit.

You should see the new diet plan I'm following now!

I'm no more than 14 days to get the body of my dreams!"

How To Tie Your Story To Your Product

If you're writing a personal story after talking about how you had a problem and used a product to solve the problem, then ask them if they would like to get the same results and then recommend the product to them as the only way they can get similar results or if they would like to use the same product that gave you the results you just shared with them and then you will add a call-to-action saying that they should click to get the same product.

With regards to case studies, and others, you will tell them the results someone has got with your product then you will ask them to get your product to get a similar result and then add your call-to-action.

Then for the 3 M's of content, you can tell them that you don't want them to keep making the same mistake that you just talked about in the story or believing the myths or misconceptions that have stopped them from achieving their goal. Then you tell them that you're offering them the right way to get results and then add the call-to-action to click and get your product.

Note: The above examples are not live copies as the products used are not real products. They're just samples or temples to help you comprehend better.